TAKE CONTROL OF YOUR LIFE

Be the protagonist of your own life!

Written by Christophe Peiffer
Translated by Ciaran Traynor

Health and Wellbeing 50MINUTES.com

TAKE CONTROL OF YOUR LIFE

- **Problem**: when you feel like you have lost control of your life, how can you get it back?
- **Aim**: many people dream of taking control of their lives, without really knowing how to get there. Each of us may be forced to take on this challenge at some point, and so this book aims to give you the keys to take the first steps down your new path in life.
- **FAQs:**
  - How can you tell if you need to take (back) control of your life?
  - Change scares me. How can I overcome this fear?
  - How can I get out of my comfort zone?
  - What can I use to help me take control of my life?
  - How can I actually go about doing this?
  - How can I find the time to take control of my life?
  - I have a lot of plans that are really just vague ideas. What can I do to make them a reality?
  - Do I need to question everything?

Unlike the French director Étienne Chatiliez's film, life is anything but a long, quiet river. You may sometimes have the unpleasant feeling that you are struggling through life rather than being the main actor. It is a little like being on one of those airport travellators, watching the scenery go by while actually not moving. Taking control of your life means getting off the travellator and walking with your own two feet, fully aware of where you are going and channelling your energy towards something meaningful.

To start with, take a look at your life. Imagine yourself climbing into a helicopter and then rising up off the ground. Suddenly, you can see your life's path stretching out in front of you.

Whether close up or from afar, your journey looks like that of many others, with its highs and lows, its good times and the times you would have preferred to do without. You probably have a classic education, after following the advice of those who "want nothing but the best for you". And so off you went to university or to learn that interesting trade which you idealised. As a result, there is a good chance that you have found a job loosely related to your studies and that you have begun to trade your time for your employer's money.

Your personal life is no doubt rather similar. Yet one beautiful morning you woke up with this unpleasant feeling that you have missed out on something and are not living the life that you pictured for yourself. It is like a call from the deepest part of your being, a grave, intense whisper that takes you completely by surprise: "It's time to take control of your life!" But how can you go about doing this? That is where this book comes in: it aims to help you to make a fresh start by listening to yourself and paying attention to the values that you hold dear.

WHY HAVE YOU LOST CONTROL OF YOUR LIFE?

OTHER PEOPLE'S INFLUENCE

It cannot be denied that education plays a vital role in how we take our lives into our own hands. You should not judge your parents for the way they raised you. It is natural that they wanted to share their vision of the world with you and, not counting a few rare cases, they probably did their best with the means that they had. Moreover, most of the time, they took an active role in the different choices that you were faced with. This is neither a bad thing, nor a good thing; they just unconsciously projected their own desires on to you. They only had your best interests at heart – they believed that you shared their values. After all, they made you! When they think of your personality, it is a bit like their "mini-me". It therefore seems obvious to them that what would have been or would be good for them is obviously good for you too.

Another influence is probably one of the worst poisons of modern society: television. Nowadays, babies are assailed by a continuous stream of television programmes as soon as they are big enough to sit on a couch. As Patrick Le Lay said in 2004, while he was the head of TF1 (French TV channel), "what we sell to Coca Cola is available human brain time"[1] (Les associés d'EIM, 2004). This space is essential if compa-nies want to make us buy a certain product while under the

---

1. This quotation has been translated by 50Minutes.com.

illusion we decided to buy it ourselves, or even if they want to somehow influence the way we see the world, thereby denying us our critical thinking skills. Is there anything more passive than watching a screen where we are spoon-fed supposedly entertaining or informative images? This addiction to an object which sucks up your potential to develop, your creativity and your potential to create stimulating projects causes you to lose control of your life.

In additions to these huge influences on your life, there are others such as:

- **Careers advisors**, who can steer an individual based on some grades on a piece of paper. This implies that "your (professional) life is determined by what you do". Does who you are even matter? Best to forget about that question: it is too complicated for them and not their priority.
- **Friends who "want nothing but the best for you"** and who, a bit like parental figures, are full of good intentions when it comes to helping you. And so you will be treated to a flood of well-meaning advice in the pub such as "you have to", "you should" or "if I were you".
- **Your partner,** who influences you with their very presence. However, do not take this the wrong way: this does not mean that he or she is the root of the problem, it just means that your bond can lead to situations such as compromises. For example, you want to go to the cinema, but your partner would rather go out for dinner, and so you find a compromise to keep both of you happy.

LOSING SIGHT OF WHO YOU REALLY ARE

All these figures can, to a certain extent, create a sort of space or rift which slowly moves you further and further away from who you really are. If this sounds familiar, you may be feeling out of step with your deepest feelings, the part of yourself where:

- all your hopes and dreams for your life can be found;
- your true needs are illuminated with a brilliant light;
- you have abilities in certain areas that others do not;
- you take an immense pleasure in being in contact with what makes you tick;
- you are aware that you were made for something other than what you are doing today;
- you have the feeling that you can contribute to something "bigger";
- you are intuitively aware of the meaning of your life.

This part of you is always somewhere within you, and it will sometimes appear with a message. This message is your Calling.

YOUR CALLING

Losing sight of who you are is a result; it is the final step of a long process involving a mixture of these previously-discussed influences, certain unconscious defence mechanisms that make you think that "taking control of your life is risky", or even getting trapped in a kind of comfort zone in your everyday habits.

For all that, you slowly begin to perceive a range of little signs, which are trying to tell you what meaning you should give to your life. And the more you try to repress them, the stronger they become. They crop up again and again under different guises. It is a bit like a call, a little voice which grows stronger and stronger and whispers existential questions in your ear:

- Why do I always meet the same toxic people?
- I just can't get this right! What's wrong with me?
- That's been six months now that my lower back is sore. I should probably get that checked out...
- Wow! That's the third time I've come across an article that sums up exactly what I've been thinking. I wonder what that means?
- How can I get motivated by what I do?

These kinds of questions never end. But if we give ourselves the time, anyone can pay attention to this deep, primal Calling and heed its message.

LEARNING TO STEER YOUR LIFE

FORGET OBJECTIVES: FOCUS ON PROJECTS

There is a wealth of personal development books which hail objectives as the holy grail of life. In a way, setting objectives, with the help of SMART, SWOT and SCORE techniques, has become the be all and end all of personal development. It is as though not having an objective is a worrying problem in itself.

Having a few objectives to focus your energy is undeniably useful. I myself use them with my clients because, as an integral part of any coaching process, they allow you to determine a course to take and provide you with certain satisfaction criteria to boot. These criteria will guide you throughout your journey.

For all that, from the point of view of taking your life in hand, having projects allows you to satisfy one of the fundamental human needs: self-fulfilment. However, you cannot just start any old project. Your projects must involve the holy trinity of happiness: Pleasure, Commitment and Meaning. Research done in positive psychology, particularly that of Martin Seligman (psychology researcher and professor at the University of Pennsylvania), has shown that happiness or subjective well-being is conditioned by the pleasure that we feel at accomplishing meaningful tasks that we are fully committed to. Let us take a look at these three components:

- **Pleasure**. Often associated with a positive emotion,

pleasure is a feeling that we have when we experience a situation that stimulates our senses. For example, we can take pleasure in watching the sun set, smelling a sweet scent, touching silky-smooth skin, eating a carefully-prepared meal or listening to spellbinding music. Pleasure is therefore essentially dependent on external stimuli and cannot fulfil us all by itself. That being said, making plans which will give you pleasure is a good base if you wish to take control of your life.

- **Commitment**. The second essential component which should be included in a project is your commitment to it. Committing yourself to a project means being able to put all your energy into it without feeling drained. On the contrary, the more committed you are, the more your energy increases. You will feel stimulated to the point of losing your grasp of time, space and self-perception. You will use your abilities to their full potential and your focus will be optimal. Nothing else exists apart from the thing you are committed to. Here are a few examples of projects favouring this flow (in psychology, flow is the mental state of a person who is completely concentrated on what they are doing), as it is called by its creator Mihály Csíkszentmihályi:
  - writing a book,
  - painting a picture,
  - taking on a sporting challenge,
  - preparing for an event,
  - learning to play an instrument,
  - doing something for charity,
  - working with others on a stimulating project.
- **Meaning**. The final essential element of every good

project is the meaning you accord it. This is perhaps even the most important element to consider once you decide to take control of your life. If you want to find meaning in your project or in your life more generally, ask yourself the following question: "Why am I doing what I am doing?" The "why" will instantly connect you to the end point of your project, with its ultimate goal. Do not get the wrong idea though – an answer will not just leap out at you. This demands some time for reflection, so you can go to the deepest part of your being and discover what has meaning for you. To help you in this task, here are some questions which will allow you to find the holy grail in your quest for meaning:

- Why are you doing this project?
- Why is it important to you?
- (Following on from the previous question) What is even more important?
- (Following on from the previous question) What do you get out of it?
- (Following on from the previous question) How does that contribute to the world around you?

Now, answer the question "Why are you doing this project?" in five to nine words.

As you can see, taking control of your life begins with creating a meaningful project which you are fully committed to and which gives you pleasure. Here is a tool that may help you to lay the groundwork of a project:

<table>
<tr><td colspan="3">Generally...</td></tr>
<tr><td>PLEASURE</td><td>COMMITMENT</td><td>MEANING</td></tr>
<tr><td>... what gives you pleasure in life?</td><td>... what activities do you fully express yourself in?</td><td>... what is important for you in your life?</td></tr>
</table>

What link can you find between all the answers that you have given to the questions above?

List five possible projects which correspond to the link above.

-
-
-
-
-

Classify them according to the holy trinity of happiness: Pleasure, Commitment, Meaning.

THE FUNDAMENTALS OF TAKING CONTROL OF YOUR LIFE

Encourage optimism

Optimism is a way of perceiving the world around us. Positive psychology (the branch of psychology which focuses on the strengths and virtues of human beings) tells us that it is also the tendency to look on the bright side of things. As the idiom goes, optimism means seeing your glass as half full and not half empty.

The optimist sees opportunities where the pessimist sees nothing but problems. The former thinks in a way which helps them not to see the world through rose-tinted glasses, but to see it just a little bit brighter. Here are a few examples of optimistic thinking:

- "The world is full of opportunities which are within my reach."
- "I have not failed. I have simply learned what not to do next time."
- "I succeeded because I made full use of my talents and abilities."
- "Other people are potential partners rather than probable enemies."
- "The impermanence of life gives me the courage to continue my journey in spite of the difficulties."

The optimist does not deny the difficulties of existence. They also go through difficult times, but they manage to put them into perspective, telling themselves that these setbacks are only temporary, and evaluate their responsibility in events.

Let us suppose that you have to participate in a sports competition at the weekend and you have not reached the objective that you wanted to. An optimistic person would find a rational explanation for this failure ("I couldn't get myself ready like I wanted to because I had to deal with more work than usual"), while a pessimist would make it into the worst thing that has ever happened to them, see themselves as completely responsible for their failure and view it as a definitive setback.

By practicing this new "life philosophy", you will be quicker to seize the opportunities which present themselves to you and you will soon feel better about yourself.

Accept change

You may have already thought as much, but it should be emphasised all the same: taking control of your life requires making several changes in your current life. After all, if you are currently reading this book, that means that your life has slipped away from you, at least in part, or it has never really been under your control and you want to change this.

In spite of this, you still need to be aware that you are developing in at least one environment, in connection with different people, in a way that you know very (or perhaps even too) well. This formula (you + environment + individuals + relationships + functioning) forms what is called a system. A system is therefore a collection of elements which interact strongly enough with one another to make up a whole which can only be described by considering the different elements separately. In this view, teams, companies and work communities are defined as open systems: they interact with an environment (Millet, 2011).

Among the principles or laws governing these systems, there is one which will almost certainly show up and will have a direct influence on you if you are committed to taking control of your life: the principle of homeostasis. This concept, which comes from biology, shows that all systems tend to reduce the variations that they have and maintain them within acceptable limits. An open system has regulation mechanisms which allow it to stay in a stable state in all circumstances, even when the environment changes. These constant regulations allow the system to survive and support itself (*ibid.*). Therefore, when it has to suffer constraints or forces encouraging it to change, the system invariably returns to how it was before this attempt to change. Below are a few situations where the principle of homeostasis will play a part:

- **[Biology]** You catch a cold; your body produces white blood cells and increases its temperature to combat the virus in an attempt to rebalance itself. This is the principle of homeostasis.
- **[Business]** A department-wide reorganisation is announced at work. A social movement begins to preserve the social benefits which may disappear after this change. Once again, the principle of homeostasis plays a large role here.

- **[Family]** Sometimes, a new arrival in a family (a baby, a grandparent) can create tensions, because the family balance has been broken. In the same way, a child leaving home can sometimes lead to tension in a couple, because the family dynamic has been unbalanced by the son or daughter leaving the nest. If the people who stay cannot find balance, the system may fall apart.
- **[Personal life]** You want to take control of your life. This is probably going to create some turbulence in the system that you have with your environment, your habits, your relationships and how you function. This means that procrastination, avoidance behaviour, excuses and self-sabotage are all signs encouraging you to keep going and showing you that you are going through change. At the end of the day, this is therefore almost a good thing, if you take it as nothing more than information and do not get too caught up in it. The next step is knowing what to do with this information.

Make choices

Another essential element in the process of taking (back) control of your life is the notion of choice. As we have just seen, taking your life into your own hands involves making several changes in your everyday habits. In order to do so, you are going to have to make some decisions. For some people, this is a terrifying thought. However, it is thanks to the different choices that you will make that you will slowly begin to take (back) the reins of your own life. However, you have to be patient, because these decisions will all add up help you to get back to an existence that is in line with your values.

A choice means deciding on one option over all the rest. We often think that we have a choice when we are given two options. However, in this specific scenario we are not facing a choice, but a dilemma. The real choice only begins when three options are presented to you. The difference, although minimal in terms of numbers, is significant on the psychological level.

Dilemmas lead to an unpleasant feeling, because by opting for one of two options, we cannot shake the feeling that we have lost something, instead of being happy about what we have actually chosen. At the end of the day, whatever option you choose, you will be left with mixed feelings. A psychological phenomenon known as cognitive dissonance (conflict between two mental processes which are, in theory, incompatible) takes over and eases this feeling of frustration by overestimating the value of the chosen option and underestimating that of the rejected option. Balance is therefore ensured. In this way, you can save a lot of mental energy by voluntarily putting yourself into a situation with a "real" choice. Therefore, if you are facing a dilemma with only two ways out, your first task is to create a third option. This could be a combination of the first two options or, if you have a particularly creative mind, a completely new option.

WHAT SHOULD I DO WHEN I CANNOT AVOID A DILEMMA?

If you are being tormented by a dilemma, rather than looking at the question based on the advantages and disadvantages of both options, ask yourself what you

Become proactive rather than reactive

The final fundamental principle if you want to take your life into your own hands is being proactive! This attitude will make you into an opportunity magnet – someone who creates their own luck.

According to the American businessman and keynote speaker Stephen R. Covey, being proactive means recognising the fact that, as humans, we are responsible for our own lives (Covey, 2005). We have the opportunity to act based on the decisions that we make: the more we make these decisions in full awareness of our actions, the more we can be proactive.

Proactive individuals draw their resources from a bottomless well within themselves; in other words, they try to solve their problems themselves before turning to external help. Moreover, proactive individuals do not hesitate to ask for help when they believe it necessary to accomplish their project. They are very aware of their values and place complete trust in them, and manage to take a step back when it comes to making a decision. Finally, generally speaking, proactive people concentrate their efforts on things which depend on them and which they are responsible for, without wasting time on things they cannot change.

Reactive individuals, on the other hand, are dependent on external circumstances when it comes to their mood, their emotions, their times and their decisions. Their references and markers in life are external, and so they generally put other people's values and opinions before their own. As a result, it is a bit like giving the remote control for your life to a third party. This person therefore has considerable power over your life by playing with all the different buttons. Finally, reactive people often exhaust themselves by trying to change situations which they have no influence over.

We can illustrate these two tendencies with an example: no matter how hard you try, you just cannot manage to finish a particular project. There are two responses to this:

- A reactive person would tend to say that it is so-and-so's fault, or it is because of the situation or the weather, or blame themselves by thinking of a hundred and one things they could have done or not done.
- A proactive person would take a step back to get an overall look at the situation, analysing it with a cool head and noting what they could change if they ever happen to do a similar project in the future. They will be able to distinguish between the external and internal problems which caused the project to fail. In any case, they will consider this disappointment as an experience which will help them to grow and develop.

This concept encourages you to acknowledge your individual responsibility in the course of your own life, although this is not always easy to admit. There are a number of arguments, some of which are very legitimate, which can throw this theory off. Among them is the argument which takes into account the elements which are not directly under your control (changing someone else's behaviour, for example) or which are completely uncontrollable (such as your past or an accident). How can we champion being proactive when there are so many external factors to take into account?

Here are three ways of reacting proactively to three different types of problems (*ibid.*):

- **The problem is directly controllable**. It may be a situation directly concerning your environment, your behaviour, your abilities or your beliefs. The proactive action would therefore be to change your general habits.
- **The problem is indirectly controllable**. It could, for example, be linked to someone else's behaviour. In this case, the proactive action would be to change your way of communicating with this person in order to get your message across. The result is far from guaranteed, but you will have done what you had the power to change. If that does not work, move on to the next point.
- **The problem is uncontrollable**. It is either something which is no longer under your control (your past, for example) or a situation which, in spite of your proactiveness, does not end the way you want it to. In this case, you still have the power to be proactive and change the way you see things. This is the stage where the notion of letting go takes on its full meaning.

<u>**In summary**</u>

If you want to take control of your life, begin by doing projects which mean something to you, which you are committed to and which give you pleasure. To do so, you will have to accept some changes in your life, particularly by making choices and being proactive rather than reactive.

HOW CAN YOU STAY IN CONTROL OF YOUR LIFE?

VALUES: THE ULTIMATE KEY TO STAY ON COURSE

Gary was in a rather rocky period of professional transition. He did not understand why he was finding it so difficult to get a job and did not even know what he wanted to or could do. He had always been active and productive, and so he could not explain why he felt he had lost control over his life. After taking a long, hard look at his wants and needs, it turned out that Gary was going through some internal conflict. One of the values that had driven him throughout the first part of his career was Money, a value hammered into him during his upbringing due to the unstable economic climate.

Nevertheless, after several prosperous years, this transitional period highlighted the change that had taken place in his value system. After identifying and ordering the values which now drive him, he realised that Money, while still important to him, had now moved to the bottom of his priorities. Others had moved up to take its place, including the wish to help others. Some time later, Gary opened up a café-bakery and took great pleasure in feeding his customers. He realised that he considers satisfying basic human needs a very worthwhile cause.

Your values are therefore a very reliable compass to stay on track in your life. Now that you are flying the plane, you just need to keep on course to move forward.

However, knowing your values, and more specifically your value system, is not as obvious as it might appear. Of course, you may already have a relatively good idea of what is important to you in life. Nevertheless, you may not have examined your current priorities in this part of your life. After all, even if our fundamental values remain more or less the same over the course of our lives, they may change based on the period that we are going through. A new value might even take the place of an old one. All this makes up the value dynamic.

Here is a three-stage tool that will help you to explore your values a little more right here and right now: the value ladder.

- **Step 1: determine what is important in your life**
  The first step is to use the table below in order to identify and list – in three different contexts – the things that you like, that you are looking for and that are important to you, as well as those that you do not like, that you avoid or that bother you.
  You will have noticed that we have still not touched on values. The idea here is to be as spontaneous as possible. You can write down key words, groups of words or full sentences if they come to you naturally. I have arbitrarily chosen professional and personal environments and will leave you to choose the last context which you feel is important in your life.
  Give yourself the time to reflect and become aware of all these things that you are enthusiastic about, that you

hear, that you see, that you live with, that attract you, that you feel good doing and that are important to you. You can do this for yourself or for others, by yourself or in a group. If something makes you feel this way, a resounding "YES" will roar out from the deepest part of your being.

Similarly, take a step back and think about everything that you hate, that makes your hair stand on end and that you try to avoid: everything that makes your body scream out "NO".

PERSONAL LIFE	What I like, what I am looking for, what is important to me	• • • • • • ...
	What I don't like, what I avoid, what bothers me, what I do not agree with	• • • • • • ...
PROFESSIONAL LIFE	What I like, what I am looking for, what is important to me	• • • • • • ...
	What I don't like, what I avoid, what bothers me, what I do not agree with	• • • • • • ...
(YOUR CHOICE OF CONTEXT)	What I like, what I am looking for, what is important to me	• • • • • • ...
	What I don't like, what I avoid, what bothers me, what I do not agree with	• • • • • • ...

- **Step 2: make a list of your values**

  After listing all of these elements which attract or repulse you, the idea is now to group them into value families. In other words, you have to gather the elements that you like, that you are looking for and that are important to you together with those that you do not like, that bother you and which correspond to the same value. You therefore have to group them under a single name which corresponds to a value/anti-value pair. Here are some examples:

- ◦ "I like to use my time the way I want to" and "I don't like feeling boxed in by rigid guidelines" can be classified under the shared value 'Freedom'.
- ◦ "I am looking for a transparent relationship" and "I cannot stand hypocrisy, backstabbing and underhanded people" can go under the shared value 'Trust'.
- ◦ "It is important for me to respect society's rules" and "Seeing some of the things my colleagues do bothers me" can be put under the shared value 'Justice'.

The shared value is the one which suits you. However, sometimes the same elements grouped by two individuals correspond to two similar but different values. The first example could also come under 'Independence'.
To help you in this task, here is a table where you can find some common values. Obviously, this is far from an exhaustive example. Why not add some of your own values to it?

VALUE TABLE				
Humility	Creation	Freedom	Progress	Trust
Money	Discovery	Loyalty	Family	Fairness
Choice	Disinterest	Mastery	Ecology	Balance
Friendship	Learning	Originality	Contribution	Evolution
Help	Exchange	Opening-mindedness	Construction	Productivity
Diversity	Efficacy	Sharing	Responsibility	Honour
Authenticity	Commitment	Participation	Innovation	Humour
Elegance	Enrichment	Pleasure	Intimacy	Independence
Aestheticism	Independence	Progression	Integrity	Health
Building	Recognition	Service	Justice	Security
Wellbeing	Leadership	Self-respect	Success	Sincerity
Happiness	Generosity	Mutual respect	Transmission	Solidarity
Change	Relational qualities	Success	Team work	A job well done
Tolerance	Creativity	Harmony	Order	Peace
...	...	...	...	...

- **Step 3: compare your values two by two**
  If you want to establish your value ladder, you have to compare your individual values. First, ask yourself which of the first two values is the most important one on the list. Give this value a point. Then move on to the first and third value, then the first and fourth, and so on, giving one point to the winner each time.

Next, take the second value to compare to the third, then to the fourth, and so on, and give one point to each value that seems the most important to you. Once you have compared all the values to one another, all you need to do is count up the scores. Obviously, the value with the most points is your most important value.

If you cannot decide between two values, you can either give each of them one point (for the most important values) or give neither of them a point (for the least important values).

For example:

VALUES	POINTS	TOTAL POINTS	FINAL SCALE
Commitment	0 1 0	1	Friendship
Freedom	1 1 0	2	Freedom
Transmission	0 0 0	0	Commitment
Friendship	1 1 1	3	Transmission
...	...	...	...

If you keep doubting one particular value, ask yourself the following question: "If I have this value, what would be even more important to me?" The answer to this question is therefore a higher-level value. If there is no answer which comes to you right away, you can be sure that this is the value which is most important to you.

WHAT SHOULD YOU EXPECT NOW THAT YOU HAVE TAKEN YOUR LIFE INTO YOUR OWN HANDS?

And there you go – you now have a beautiful little compass that you have just made yourself. This is a valuable, unique tool. If you use it every day to take control of your life – while following the advice in this guide – you will soon see changes with benefits you cannot even begin to comprehend. Therefore, pay attention to the positive effects described above, in case you suddenly feel like letting go of your life again and watching it slip away from you…

So many opportunities

Professional and personal opportunities will now be coming at you from all angles. No, they have not magically multiplied; your new state of mind has just made you more open to all these new chances to commit yourself to stimulating, meaningful projects. The other secondary effect of this opening to opportunities is that you will attract people with similar ways of thinking. Imagine what you can do with people who have just as many opportunities in their lives and just as much passion to seize them!

The power to create your own luck

When you were just a spectator to your own life, you had the luxury of being able to blame your problems on everything from bad luck to the whole world being against you. What an easy life! Now that you have taken matters into your own hands, things get a bit more complicated. The changes in your daily life will have encouraged you to open yourself up to others and yourself. As a result, you are more receptive than before and, just like your opportunities, you will find that luck is on your side far more often than before.

Goodbye self-sabotage!

When you were still letting your life pass you by, you were completely free to mess up a project, relationship or interesting opportunity. Now that you have taken (back) control, there is a good chance that you are beginning to succeed at what you set out to do. Taking into account your new ability to heed warning signs and make carefully-considered decisions, you will now make better choices. So watch out: there is a real danger that your projects might grow more and more successful! Moreover, even if a project does not quite work out, you are now in a position to turn it into a learning experience to avoid the same pitfalls in the future.

A new sense of independence

Without even realising it, the road that you have gone down to take control of your life has given you a clear conscience (with regard to yourself, others and situations), allowed you to have fluid, spontaneous relationships and, most importantly of all, helped you to pay attention and respond to your needs. So there you have it: you have discovered the key to happiness!

FAQS

HOW CAN YOU TELL IF YOU NEED TO TAKE (BACK) CONTROL OF YOUR LIFE?

As soon as you notice signs in your life that the path you have taken does not really suit you, it is time to act. These signs may manifest themselves as a recurrent sense of uneasiness, unexplained chronic pains, repeated "coincidences" relating to the same thing, different encounters all with the same message concerning you, and so on. All of these elements should draw your attention to the fact that you may have lost control over your life and that it is time to take matters into your own hands.

CHANGE SCARES ME. HOW CAN I OVERCOME THIS FEAR?

Unfortunately, change is something you just have to accept, because nothing stays the same in life. Being afraid of change is like being afraid of day and night, the seasons or the weather.

Concerning the changes in your own life, do not think that you have to deny who you are: consider this change a way to become the person that you will be, the person that you aspire to be. Fear is a feeling that warns us of danger. However, in this case, what is the danger? Once you have identified it, you will be in a better position to minimise its impact on you, and perhaps will even be able to make it disappear.

HOW CAN I GET OUT OF MY COMFORT ZONE?

You need your comfort zone to recharge your batteries, feel safe and, of course, comfortable. However, there is another area next to your comfort zone: your effort zone, where you can explore new horizons, find new resources you did not even know you had, and discover new ways to grow. Rather than considering leaving your comfort zone as a one way trip, think of it as a day out. There is no reason you cannot explore uncharted territory and come back to your safe place from time to time to recharge your batteries.

WHAT CAN I USE TO HELP ME TAKE CONTROL OF MY LIFE?

The main things to take your life into your own hands are your internal values, which are unique to you. You can also use your talents and the situations in which you are in your element.

Two other pillars you can lean on are your intuition and your pleasure. Intuition is that little voice which sometimes whispers very sensible things to you, which you stick to until it is muffled by all of your mental filters. Pleasure is that pleasant feeling that connects you to your inner child.

HOW CAN I ACTUALLY GO ABOUT DOING THIS?

There are a lot of things you can do! For example, you could try taking a break to listen to what that little voice is whispering to you and think about what it has to say, or begin therapy in order to get a better idea of your needs and values, or even get a life coach to guide you throughout the process.

It is also important to take initiatives that give you pleasure. In this regard, it is extremely important to listen to how you feel when doing things.

Why not make the most of it to go off on a trip by yourself, which will make you experience new things? You will expand your horizons and take stock of yourself.

You could also set yourself a little daily challenge. This will not only make you more dynamic and increase your sense of satisfaction, but it will also help you to discover certain things about yourself that you did not even suspect. In a similar vein, do not be afraid to put yourself in situations where you have to make choices. Most importantly, doubt everything except yourself!

HOW CAN I FIND THE TIME TO TAKE CONTROL OF MY LIFE?

You do not need time to take control of your life. Going from being a spectator to an actor is really nothing more than a change in mentality. And the show does not stop. That being said, if you decide to really go for it, you have to give yourself the time to accomplish this quest. Rome was not built in a day! Be patient, and enjoy each step of the way.

I HAVE A LOT OF PLANS THAT ARE REALLY JUST VAGUE IDEAS. WHAT CAN I DO TO MAKE THEM A REALITY?

There are several options open to you. The first is to get help from professionals who specialise in this sort of thing. Another is to ask yourself what you have not let go of in your past and which is preventing you from advancing today. You could also begin with a little project, and then another, and then another, referring to the Pleasure, Commitment, Meaning trinity each time to guide you in your journey.

DO I NEED TO QUESTION EVERYTHING?

That depends on several factors:

- how committed you are to taking control of your life;
- how honestly you can analyse yourself;
- how motivated you are to explore grey areas;
- how uncomfortable you feel in your current life;
- how much you can bear the difficulties you are currently facing.

In any case, there are two types of change, each with its own benefits and risks:

- Change 1 will allow you to make several modifications to your life to become a little more independent while still keeping a sense of balance. The benefit is a (possibly illusory?) feeling of security. The risk is coming back sooner or later to your current situation with all the complications that this entails.
- Change 2 is a paradigm shift: a complete turnaround towards the new you. The benefit is that this type of personal development is long-lasting.

FURTHER READING

BIBLIOGRAPHY

- Covey, S. (2004) *The 7 Habits of Highly Successful People.* New York: Simon and Schuster.
- Millet, O. (2011) *Manuel de formation à l'intervention systémique en entreprise.* (n.p.): (n.p.).
- Peiffer, C., Roland, E., Aubry, K. and Boutin, A.-C. (2012) Les valeurs. *Le Blog des rapports humains. fr.* [Online]. [Accessed 18 July 2017]. Available from: <http://www.leblogdesrapportshumains.fr/les-valeurs-ebook-a-telecharger/>

ADDITIONAL SOURCES

- Grenville-Cleave, B. (2012) *Introducing Positive Psychology: A Practical Guide (Introducing...).* London: Icon Books Ltd.
- Hopkins, B. (2016) *7 Steps to Taking Control of Your Life.* (n.p.): Self-published.

IMPROVE YOUR GENERAL KNOWLEDGE

IN A BLINK OF AN EYE !

www.50minutes.com

www.50minutes.com

Ebook EAN: 9782808000239

Paperback EAN: 9782808000246

Legal Deposit: D/2017/12603/439

Cover: © Primento

Digital conception by Primento, the digital partner of publishers.